WITHDRAWN
UTSA LIBRARIES

Preparing to Be Happy

Books by T. Alan Broughton

Poetry

In the Face of Descent
Far From Home
Dreams Before Sleep
Preparing to Be Happy

Novels

A Family Gathering
Winter Journey
The Horsemaster
Hob's Daughter

Limited Editions

Adam's Dream
The Others We Are

Preparing to Be Happy

poems by
T. Alan Broughton

Carnegie Mellon University Press
Pittsburgh 1988

LIBRARY
The University of Texas
at San Antonio

Acknowledgments

Acknowledgment is made to the editors of the following magazines in which many of these poems first appeared:

Beloit Poetry Journal: "Overture"
Chariton: "Beyond Change"
"Brook Changes"
"A Simple Death"
"Vacant Lot"
Confrontation: "Recreation Hour"
"African Violets"
"A Curse for Dictators"
Denver Quarterly: "Family History"
Kansas Quarterly: "Caretaker"
The Literary Review: "Ice Fisher"
New England Review/Breadloaf Quarterly: "Summer Killer"
North by Northeast: "Cicadas"
Northeast: "For Leviathan"
Poets On: "Elements"
"Brief Meeting"
"Measurements"
"Old Boy"
Quarterly West: "Don Giovanni in Retirement"
The Reaper: Preparing to Be Happy"
Seneca Review: "Freeze"
Tar River Poetry: "A Winter"
Three Rivers Poetry Journal: "Amish Market"
"The Woman Under Us"

The following poems were published in Poetry, CXLIX, No. 5 (February 1987): "Heroics" "Aeneas Through The Looking Glass" Copyright, Modern Poetry Association.

"Ice Fisher" received a Fifth Annual Angoff Award from *The Literary Review.*

The publication of this book is supported by grants from the National Endowment for the Arts in Washington, D.C., a Federal agency, and by the Pennsylvania Council on the Arts.

Carnegie Mellon University Press books are distributed by Harper and Row, Publishers.

Library of Congress Catalog Card Number 87-71456
ISBN 0-88748-060-8
ISBN 0-88748-061-6 Pbk.
Copyright©1988 by T. Alan Broughton
All rights reserved
Printed and bound in the United States of America
First Edition

Contents

I Elements

Departure   11
Elements   12
Heroics   13
Brief Meeting   14
Measurements   15
An Old Story   16
Children of Fire   17
Inland Journey   18
Into the World   20
Evensong   28

II Evensongs

Cicadas   33
Amish Market   34
The Woman Under Us   35
Summer Killer   37
Old Boy   42
My Late Espoused   43
Speedboat   44
Family History   46
Writer at Work   48
Brook Changes   50
Vacant Lot   51
Voice in the Sky   52
Recreation Hour   53
Child's Play   54
African Violets   55
A Curse for Dictators   56
For Leviathan   58

III Winter Voices

The Other	61
Aeneas Through the Looking Glass	62
Don Giovanni in Retirement	64
A Winter	66
Caretaker	68
A Letter from Lois	70
Overture	75
Ricochet	78
A Simple Death	81
Beyond Change	84
Ice Fisher	87
Mr. Dibble Stands by the Gate	90
Preparing to be Happy	93
Freeze	97

For Gerald Costanzo

who helps to make
the making
of poems worthwhile

Que chacun examine ses pensées, il les trouvera toutes occupées au passé et à l'avenir. Nous ne pensons presque point au présent; et, si nous y pensons, ce n'est que pour en prendre la lumière pour disposer de l'avenir. Le présent n'est jamais notre fin: le passé et le présent sont nos moyens; le seul avenir est notre fin. Ainsi nous ne vivons jamais, mais nous espérons de vivre; et, nous disposant toujours à être heureux, il est inévitable que nous ne le soyons jamais.

Blaise Pascal, *Pensées*

I. Elements

Departure

From a bus window you watch
your parents. Even eyes fail
as you glance away, shamed
to stare with such longing.
How old they have become,
shoved by grief into the future.
Your mother's hands cannot stop
writhing, your father weeps
without moving his lips.
They bend under the weight
of a fallen sky. You wonder,
'Is this the couple who named me,
who taught me how to read
or enter sleep listening
to phrases from other rooms?'
These are the strangers you love.

Elements

Each earthly revelation rises, beating
its new wings through the pulse,
casting a shadow of sudden stillness.
Here memory snatches some remnant
from renewable blaze of bone and wing,
and I learn again how love permits complexities
to grow, then burns this new compound
to simple matter, changed.

My love turns quickly in a shaft of light,
leaves shattered into colors at her feet,
and all that we have known together
shines through the window of that moment.
Or as I leave my childhood home again
I see my mother's younger face,
my father sluffs his aging form
and they are what they were before I came.

Light burns in flames of tree and stone,
our bodies flickering through years,
and we touch and call out names
because one life cannot sustain
the weight of truths untouchable as air.

Heroics

"Fire on the mountain," they said, "who's going?"
We left our square dance, our summer girls.
How large the night grew when we stood
on the clubhouse porch, a gusty wind
rustling the leaves into waves that beat
on the shore of the golf course.
We could have wept for the greatness
that sharp stars, the hunger of fire had thrust upon us.
As we hunched into the truck under whipping low branches
each of us thought of our ladies waiting and waiting
long after the noble ship had gone down.

We stumbled for hours high over the lake
but never found our fire until morning.
By then it was out. Descending
I met my father rising.
I was his only son. Why shouldn't he
nod serenely once he knew
I was safe? But fury seized me.
How dare he invade my burning city,
my chance with sword in the heat of battle?
I strode away and only years later
turned my head to search for the fire where again
and again he rises, thrusting
his love toward me, the figure
a son is pushing away from,
a city in flames behind him.
But anyone knows how the hero should
lift such a man on his back.

Brief Meeting

Father of my bride,
our blood came together in name
and parted. After this morning's chance encounter
you will turn at the driveway ahead
to buildings no longer yours
but site of your childhood.
I will shake your hand
and take up my running; we will part
again with some quip of irony.
I cannot follow your stroll
deeper and deeper into the years
before I knew you, cannot be present
when your last walk is ending the future.
The final paces are measured in silence.
But I know the same grief took you
before our hands groped to say it:
some fathers and sons meet for only a moment
and memory quick as a single, firm handshake
leaves the palm shaped but hollow.

Measurements

I believe in your age as I cannot in my own.
I never held myself in two hands,
fishbone ribs and wobbly neck.
You were a kick against my palm
when your mother's flesh lay between us.
You were a creature crawling faster than you walked,
then running in tumbles of flexible bone.
At first the ball you threw would fly straight up.
You laughed soon when I flinched;
my hand burned under leather.
But I have always been the same,
as old as I ever am,
unconvinced my body shifts to fill or wash away.
Who is that person each morning staring back
where I should stand to shave?
After childhood the soul is unimpressed,
hears only the tumult of its own carpentry.

But the body insists. Knowledge grows inward
from the hands. Blindly I grope across your shoulder.
My arms clasp someone larger than I am
and only your hand fits into mine.
Now I am as old as my father was.

An Old Story

for Jack

Because the old dog could not stand
we lifted him into the car.
But he did not let his head lie down.

As the needle emptied into the vein
we rested our hands on his flank.
Slowly he laid his head down and died.

In a field near the vacant barn
you dug a hole deep enough
for fifteen of your twenty years.

You freed him of his collar,
settled his head and stroked one ear,
then wrapped the body in a blanket.

One by one you pounded the nails,
shoveled until that place was nothing
but a mound of broken soil.

In silence we stood in an evening field
in silence we watched the earth
rise up to cover the sun.

At such times as this a father
can only bear witness.

Children of Fire

From the moment of your launching,
bright tongue of sun flare
torching its own connections,
I should have known how dread
would be the thin shadow
knifing each elation of your rise

how, when you climbed higher and higher
only I would fear a fall,
left to replay the melting explosion
enhanced by the clearest blue,
white streaks marring the surface forever

how at such distance
I would not be able to touch
the face that once was small as a bud,
through all its blooming
never revealing who unfurled it

how I would lie sleepless
from wanting to hold up
the weight of your life miles above
the simple planet I have known.

But you choose to lift off
and shake my ground,
showing how lightly you take it.
See how my wondering face
tilts with your rise,
my body leans now as if to fall backwards
from your steep growing.
And where is that place you reach
when you break into light
and my stunned eyes search
each trace in a vanishing sky?

Inland Journey

I am looking for you
in long-foreclosed farms,
in bins of oats where I play
    and choke on dust while you thresh,
in mute turnings of your bed beyond the wall,
in the tremble of your voice
    when some fragment of history
    breaks from you, *lacrimae rerum*
    hidden in simple dates,
in the figure turned to stone on the platform
    who stubbornly waits for my train to depart.

Often as I sit with you
I search from island to island,
asking the faces of memory if you were there.
Are you my father if even as you talk
to the pages of your book I cannot extract
an image of younger eyes, a shape
without present shadows?

Now when you walk
weight falls heavily
from shoulders through unbending knees.
Flesh has shifted downward
obscuring an eye, blunting the once sharp lines
of chin and nose. I look for you
behind that mask, telling myself
you were the one who carried me
high over fields of wet hay,
the one who reined in horses
wild to break from their traces.

My own sons look for me.
One calls out for the echo I should make,
the other whose voice cannot yet form words
grips my finger and sucks on flesh

he does not question yet.
My bones are light but I have no wings,
my voice speaks out of an empty box
and only shakes the air.
Do not leave me alone, nothing
at my back to shore up this hollow ignorance.
When I gaze up to flyways for patterns,
listening for the cry of a flock returning,
I dread a season of silence.

Soon the afternoon sun will not bend
across your mottled hand.
We are born in a spasm of light
and eyes begin the deceptions.
Beloved, let us be blind
and dream of our last voyage
when you will ask me gently
to descend. The waves will be small here,
washing high up a shelving beach.
I will step into their drag
as you sit with hands in your lap,
the turned tide pulling you outward.

Old father, let me journey inland
with your oar on my shoulder.
Let me carry this worn memento
until even the memory of ocean
has no wrack or salt. That oar
is your hand that rests on my shoulder.

I have held two sons and a daughter
and know how long after eyes are closed
in the darkest night the hands
that held a whole small body
can clasp in fear of gravity,
love for the helpless flesh.

Into the World

1. The Pact

In the night of your second week
I held you in a room where black leaves
shivered on the walls, where moonlight
seeped into your eyes,
and at last you slept.
Your swaddled body leaned
to the curve of my bending flesh.
I am a wave that will toss and shatter
long before you are my age.
But together we breathed that night,
together our faces were stained
by shifts of light
and I made this pact:

I will change the world so no son is flung
broken-skulled on a distant beach to eat its sand;
no cells will gnaw your marrow-bone
and I will draw fevers from you with this cool palm;
I will drag Death down,
grappling with hands and teeth,
freezing my tongue to the zero of his bones;
I will fill the rooms of your house
with boxes of wisdom, each one labeled
Open When Needed, each one appropriate
for the chafing of that day;
I will leach the night of sleepless hours,
replenish the day until flowers shade your cares.

This I must swear
if peace is to walk with me
in small steps I take from room to familiar room.
But of these vows,
only this one is certain:
love is what will hold us

as I hold you now, speechless, furled in the lap
of a larger body trusted
for that moment we call sleep.

2. Silent Night

The first night I slept
without hearing your voice
I woke at dawn uncertain
who I was. Was this land
the place where I closed my eyes
or had the dreamer I become
slipped the rope and let us drift
too far upstream? Each night he tilts
the world toward the black hole
of a spring beyond memory,
and soon I will pour over that edge
to remember what I've never seen.

I stood by the doorway
listening for the scurry of your breath,
the kick of a waking foot on a slat.
My little changeling, stranger
who each morning lifts a surprised
face to a new father hovering
over the rail, did you sleep
without murmur, lulled by
the voice of your rocking heartbeat,
or did I hold too tight to the stone
of my weary flesh as I plunged into silence?

Somehow the wakers open their eyes
to light and believe in the raucous
chatter of day. I lift you
over my head and again we start
making the stuff of our dreams.

3. Child Killer

I can see you enter the baby's room
while all the house is sleeping.
Stiff and still you have lain in bed
after the usual tumble of your husband's loving,
his wordless roll into slumber.
This is all planned: the way the streetlamp
casts its purple slats across the crib,
the way that small face, plugged with a thumb,
breathes so lightly you have to hold
your ears close to the flattened nose.
You wonder if nature has already started
what you are compelled to finish,
lifting the pillow from the chair
where you rocked and nursed him,
pausing one moment to stare before
you press it down, and down
as if such miniature limbs could throw
back the airless weight, the choked voice
clamour. With eyes closed you grip
the last image of that face,
brow already dark with hair,
your family's dimpled chin.
The freight train howls
along the lake, a truck stampedes the block
hoping to make the light.
The house settles under a press
of cold sky. Your finger
searches for breath. None.
Silence. Another death.

I can even see what follows—
the drift into sleep, rising to alarm,
your reluctant groping for housecoat,
a pale lurch into the room where

you scream and collapse. None of this
has to be feigned. How terrible to see
your worst dreams in the image
of that breathless body, ragdoll carried
laxly down the stairs.

Processions. Grief. Another coffin.
The comfort of neighbors. Stoic
acceptance. The Lord giveth.
'I am still young. We keep on trying.'
Your husband stares at your clenched face
wondering what God has given him to endure—
three born, three who died, and wife
who will not relent in her need for more.

All this I see and though my heart skips
and slows at what the inner eye imagines,
though I stumble and rage in the corridors
of indignation for the helpless sleeper,
child who could not cry out at birth
like some singing bone, 'Save me, save me,'
I cannot, my sister jailed
in the same fleshly cage of time,
see deep enough to understand. I pause
at the threshold of some last room
where all could be shown
if only my hands would shove the door
which hangs ajar. I want to see why,
want to be able to know
you in that impossible moment of killing.
Galaxies loosen through stretching space.
I fear those infinite drifts.

Tonight, sister of death, mother without mercy,
I stand by my infant's bed and keep watch
on his breathing and twitch of his dreams.

His eyes flutter under thinnest lids
and I wrap my love tightly around him
to hold back the harsh and ancient light of stars.
Above him I shake the bones
of every charm and lullaby:
he must not die, he must not die.
And when my hand slips through
the jostling atoms of air, traverses
this distance packed with unseen life
I wonder, my sister, if all we have done
is sit on the opposite sides, tilting up,
then down—your love slanting to fear
of what must come and seizing death by the throat
before he makes his move, my love
in the hopeless warding. In ignorance
I turn away, in ignorance I tumble
into sleep where you and I will meet
in the cave with no pictures.

4. Baptism for a Son

The soldiers rest.
Some lean in doorframes and watch
the earth dragged over the sun,
some sleep hunched by embers
of chairs and shattered floors.
Where houses stand generals debate
the next blunt probe for death.

When I held you, and the rite
named you Christian, praised your birth
with water and oil, made holy
all possibilities of change, even to die,
I listened through quick breaths on my cheek
to echoing prayers intoned around us.
My heathen lips were sealed, but I sang

dumbly in the dark cave of hope.

A soldier climbs
tilted stairs and finds a single room intact.
A bed, a crib, and pictures smiling from their frames—
Mother and Father in rented wedding clothes,
Gramma holding a sleeping bundle of lace,
the newly baptised fragment of this home.
He lights a primus, huddles by its blue
and insufficient flame. The night collapses
around him, dark tent whose ropes and poles
were frayed by the chafing of day.

"Remember," our deacon instructed,
"when we anoint his head with water,
all that it gives—quenching thirst,
nurturing crops, but also drowning, and the huge sea
that bears us down. This is a mystery,
its names are both Life and Death,
and we pray for Grace in our coming and going."
Under a wide oak I too could chant
for your passage as she carries you
down the long aisle and back, a candle
holding your gaze while we watch.
You follow the flame that bends
and flickers ahead of your journey.
The air parts for you, you come again
to the stone where your father waits. Brief light,
now you consume the blood and body of a god.
You are Nathaniel.

In a dark field
beyond the ravaged town, a child
cannot find the ones he knows best.
They are beyond recognition.
The comfort of friends cannot touch

the place he retreated to when tides
of armies washed in and out
on tugs of their crazed moons.
But he knows his way over frosted humps of craters,
the path where his father's tractor mired.
The door to his home hangs on one hinge,
the stairs sag, but he climbs.

We gathered in a house
with friends to toast your life
with wine profane as the earth itself
and watched you crawl through legs and under chairs
purely in search of motion, following the bright path
of your eyes. Thousands of years of history,
bloody and innocent, named you as their own,
but you took that weight upstairs to your nap
and dreams as old as the human shape you wear.
You fought with sleep, kicked,
closed your eyes and tumbled into
everything you are.

The soldier wakes
to a rattle of fear. He knows
his life is an accident of strokes.
He could have died like others
winged by flying steel.
He lifts his gun.
The door swings open for a child
who does not pause to speak
to a stranger in his room. Through slats
of his crib he seizes a dark,
misshapen creature, companion of his nights.
When he is gone the soldier stares
and wonders, all his life recalls
how tightly his finger curled to the trigger,
how war was only this dream.

Child of my middle age, my terrifying joy,
each day our sun rises to the spinning edge of earth
may you be washed with its light,
may you travel through each turn into darkness
holding whatever loved charms bear you through.

5. Portrait of Nathaniel

In a blue chair
that surrounds you,
in a square of sunlit floor,
you waggle arms and legs
in delighted semaphore.
Eyes wide as if
resenting a blink,
you absorb the ruffled green
of breezy trees, the sleeping dog,
father in his perch
high on a couch.
You frown, and smile, cry out
and smile again, render
all things of this world
into babble.

We need no words.
You follow the pitch of my voice,
I read your tones—emotions ride in
on the keys of our song.
See how I lift you
now, and mere hands
bear the chanting universe—
so light, so quick.

Evensong

We play in the last hours of failing light.
In late songs of flight birds loop,
in the fields children kick or throw,
voices so distant their words fall away.
In long rallies we keep no score,
stroke a yellow ball that darkens,
fades into dusk. This father can not win
against your greater skill, and now the rhythm
of two bodies sending an object back and forth
through summer air is enough, a harmony
in light, light that is water
where trailing leaves, cries of children in flight,
splotches of sky and quavering vines
immerse us, and the ball that is nothing but motion
is the fragile center suspending every center
but its own.
        I dream each night of Giverny,
of bridges burning with dangling flowers
and an old man holding out a brush toward
a vanishing canvas, light dimming to the center
of his eyes—pale surface, wild palette crooked in his arm,
brush dipped and poised. In the moment before
his hand permits the possible touch once more,
when air washes its own light between the stroke
and the frame of vacancy, his mind vanishes
into sheer blindness. Again he knows
he will fail, the light he loves
will not hold still, again and again he will dip
the greedy brush and reach and Nothing will be
what he sees, Nothing will drown the wish.
The canvas will only hold the smear
of passage between two speeding strokes—
his mind and the world.
But across that infinite gap, his hand will stumble,
marring a surface toward its own perfection:

lilies in a sky of pond, willows
dissolving into clouds. He holds the universe
of light and breaks it outward into colors,
thinking he only gives back what he owes.

But my dreams are reflections of our games,
brief span of evenings when sun and other distant stars
flow serenely. Why call the flood of chaos
darkness? It is too much light,
light that sears so whitely the eye cannot see again
to break it into any spectrum. Two cars,
your friends, a swerve—only the slightest marring
of casual motions, but that is an end.
Not for you, not for all time, but for this summer.

Now trees cast clear shadows,
voices in that field are plucked and twang with steel,
and night comes too soon. Your eyes
have not seen death until this moment,
and you are looking at his etchings, acid
imprints hung on impenetrable walls.

With my eyes closed I can see us,
and I still dream of Giverny, and wait.
The light will dim again, and we will celebrate
the way its swirls and ripples gather for a moment
into shapes we trust enough to touch—
leaves flowing, flowers drifting through our hands.

II. Evensongs

Cicadas

In evenings of the season
when locusts left
their bodies,
I took my paper bag
from tree to tree gently
plucking the smoky
shells. The carapace clung
to wrinkled bark,
unwilling to give up.

I hoarded them
on my bedside table,
peering backwards through bulbs
of eyes, the vacant head,
ghosts a small breath
could disarrange. I was told
they could still be heard
rasping even in heat of day
but I never saw them.

Through slits in their backs
souls had escaped, singing
now, singing always into the night.
They gathered near my window
calling out to their bodies,
those frail shapes
that held them once.

Amish Market

Water on a concrete floor to lay the dust
cooled air where tubs of exploding flowers,
bread still flexing to rise through its crust,
sugary twists of crullers, warm eggs feathered with down,
hung hocks of bloody meat, bursting green cones
of corn, tomatoes splitting their sides
and plums so plump with juice the jaw ached
at their oozing stacks—all these
waited for our basket never ample enough.
And my eyes, my insatiable nose
would have all of it, all in a swimming
through bounty, mouth open in a flood
of tumbling cherries and peaches.

Who were those round faces, their stern hats
and black frocks denying such plenty?
But they smiled unfrugally,
their horses staled and flopped outside
and wagons creaked to be off again,
back to fields and spilling bins of grain.

What hollows they scooped out when they left:
stained slab, scarred tables on rickety legs,
a slithery rot of leaves where the broom
failed. Mold stank under a smirch of sun.
I have stood with empty hands in such a place,
called out sharply but never again,
fearing my own voice bouncing down,
a leaden rolling into stillness in corners
where rats cowered, where nothing good
waited to be taken home.

The Woman Under Us

While my father and mother went dancing
I hid by the cracked door
of my darkened room and watched the woman
my mother hired to sit in the parlor
lolling back on our couch, thighs splayed
and stockings rolled at her knees.
She dozed until I thought she slept,
but her head began to rock
and she hummed in a gentle moan
with her arms crossed over her breasts.
The slits of her eyes were fixed on me,
her song lifting and folding me down
till I woke in the morning curled in a bed
that did not seem my own.

My father said, "Stay out of the basement,
that's not your home."
The door to her room was ajar.
Again she was humming
and when I stood close to the crack
the air wafting out was thick
with sweet rot of earth
turned up to the sun.

I hid when someone came downstairs.
"Bella?" he called softly and knocked.
"Honey, you there?"
What I heard was a snatch of moan,
her hum of welcome. Oh, how he laughed
when he pushed the door,
and I wanted to join him.

Quietly over the cindered floor
I carried my hammering heart,
kneeled by the wall and that careless crack.

What was that low slap of hand
on flesh about? Her laugh had no pain.
On hands and knees, in mildew and dust
I heard them chant, and they beat
the drum of a headboard hard
until she cried out in unceasing breath
that flowed through every room of that rented house,
and I stood up fearful
she had died.

When I lie in fever,
when stretched pain of body
or untouchable rack of mind
screws tight enough to snap me,
I think of how I rolled deep into joy
when her low and honeyed humming began again
and the comb of the house grew fat
on that single room, the flowers
under the cherry trees blazed
from their buds, and I could have curled
forever in sleep while she rocked
the world in her wide arms.

Summer Killer

All August we thrilled to rumors.
Near the brook Alex Hunt glimpsed a figure,
ragged and stooping to drink,
and left his flyrod to run two miles
and report. Rewards were waiting,
enough to buy twenty rods.
Lovers on East Hill saw a shadow
flit through headlit brush. She barely
had time to pull up her pants before
they spun into Carl's Garage with the news.
The next day she said she wasn't sure,
"Might've been a bear or deer."
The State Police parked all day and night
by the entrance to trails or old wood roads,
smoking, eating the snacks we brought.
Four of them got lost on Hedgehog chasing
a barefoot hiker (no shoes sounded suspicious),
and we found them scattered like lost calves, bellowing.

After the first two weeks we thought we didn't care;
but he raised the ante on every gesture we made,
filled the casual evenings with bright contrasts.
You couldn't ignore what flicked in the corners of your eyes,
might pause lifting a stick of wood
to listen to crickets, the downward swirl
of a hermit thrush as if someone else
were listening beside you, listening harder
than you ever could. Because he'd killed—
tearing the fabric of every day to stand on the other side,
making it hard to know if he was the substance
casting a shadow that was you, or vice versa.
"Two more loads at least before you go,"
my dad said, and wheeling the barrow back, I shivered,
trying to ignore how even the drabbest chores
took on gravity, how even nagging
couldn't root out the beauty of danger.

He'd only performed the simplest mayhem,
our killer trapped in a summer home.
Drunk on the liquor of absent owners,
he didn't think before he fired
and blew off the side of one cop's head,
left the other to bleed to death with wounded belly.
Because they were cops and both had families
the Governor called it *A Heinous Crime*
and expanded our vocabulary.
We lowered the town hall flag to halfmast,
bought out all the shells at the hardware
left from last hunting season.

"He's in those woods for sure,"
our senator told us, "we'll have him,"
forgetting those woods spread from Champlain to Erie
if you crossed the fields at night.
Who could believe me now if I said
each one of us dreamed of crouching behind a boulder
in wet moss, stumbling across bogs at dawn, dogs
on the neighboring ridge yapping from footstep
to footstep as we looked for the hidden exit?

But I had my own furtive plans
that nothing could change, so after the firewood
was loosely stacked in its box,
after the carkeys were handed over,
I picked up the bottle I'd stashed
in the hole of the gatepost and drove
to the house where her parents
had left her in glorious isolation
for the whole night while they journeyed
to Boston. What more could you ask for?
A house made for summer only, as rustic
as any movie set, a fireplace where two hogs
could have twirled on spits,

and a bear rug as soft as a feathery bed.
Of course we'd pretended we weren't going here,
bare in the firelight, the owls outside
hooting us on, our young bodies knowing more
than their owners could ever have guessed.
If it hurt for a moment, she didn't complain,
and after the silence, after we heard the house
settle down to the cooler night air
she brought in a blanket so we could lie naked
breathing and whispering and drinking the whiskey
that turned our dizzy words liquid
before we went back to our learning.

What instinct made me leave the car
down the road? I came like a thief
to my lover's house, and praised myself
for that salvation. "Wasn't that Willy's car
in the field?" I heard her old man ask
as I crouched naked on the screened-in porch.
"I doubt it," she murmured, trying hard
to keep her syllables firm. "What
in the world are you bundled like that for?"
her mother asked shrilly. She must have been lumped
like a squaw in that blanket, my clothes
and hers clutched to her body. "I'm naked,"
she snapped, and after her angry heals pummeled
the floor, those small feet flapping
up the stairs, her father, his own tongue slurring,
muttered, "Clara, I'll never understand my daughter."

That wasn't my problem. I dreaded
the sudden flick of light, his need
to come out and look at the stars.
He poked the fire, she asked for a drink,
and slowly I pushed out the screen, blessing
its rot and the way it tore easily

out of the frame. "Honey," she was calling,
"did you hear something out there?"
but I wasn't waiting, hung by my fingers
and prayed as I tried to remember
how close to the cliff their house was perched,
and dropped. Not far, but my knees
buckled me flat on my ass, enough to imbed
some pebbles. I was moving into the trees
away from cliffs when the light went on
and she began screaming, "He's here,
he's here, he tried to break in."

I won't tell you what my feet looked like
after five miles of hiking away from the roads,
scratches all over my body from alders
and spruce bows. I circled our house
for hours with my clouds of mosquitoes
waiting for parents to fall asleep,
cursing my father's insomnia.
The phone should have rung or police have arrived
in search of the ripper of screens, despoiler
of daughters. I hunched by the woodshed,
knees to my chest, back surrendered to bloodsuckers.
Stars were blinking in layers, I shivered
in rhythm to the quivering sheets of aurora.
I had to wonder if all this was worth it,
but no matter how numb the punished body
I answered I'd do it again and again
even if she weren't the one,
and couldn't help praising beginnings.

When the last light went out I stood
and someone stood with me.
But wherever I looked directly
nothing was there, only tree trunks
and shadows. I moved, and he moved

with me, I stopped and he waited.
The dark house was mine for the taking,
but the whole world spread out and held up the sky.
We could have kept walking together,
not seeing each other. We chose
to part at the door to the cottage
and I'm sure he nodded, I waved,
and I would have spoken except I knew
we would follow each other forever
through woods and fields and streets of strange cities.

I answered all riddles. The car had run out of gas,
that bundle of clothes had been left at her house after tennis.
"We've had such a scare," her mother told mine.
"That killer, we're sure he was trying
to break in and rob us, and what
would have happened if we'd stayed in Boston?"
We never had chances like that again.
The summer ended, as usual, in tears,
a season's passing mourned for that moment,
but how could I grieve for long?
I'd gotten away with all I had wanted.

They found him that winter in Arizona.
He'd taken to bragging in barrooms.
They put him away, didn't kill him.
I kept my mouth shut so they never found me,
and still I'm taking whatever I can,
hoping I won't have to shoot my way out,
and trying before I leave each house
to give everything back.

Old Boy

At noon on a February lawn
my guide describes a new dorm
and I want to lash my fist against its thickened panes
because I cannot blame these ragged trees,
heaved sidewalks, clapboard homes
for marriages I did not keep, children
left to walk back through the night
to find a cellar hole, scorched timbers for a room.

Late afternoon, I see beyond the gym
an edge of wood, the icy stream
where again and again the first woman took me in
while ground beneath us froze or thawed
or pulled leaves deeper into sod;
but why go tumbling across new lovers?
I turn my back, search for a glass of wine
and talk of stoves, of keeping houses warm.

That night, my stories of nostalgia told to anyone,
I lie and listen for a voice
to tell me where I was, recount
the fable I never tell myself.
I hear the shuddering of a pipe,
my housemates' heels hollowing out
the last steps toward dreams,
then silence measures its store of vacancy.
Only the heart continues to speak
in wordless iambs.

My Late Espoused

The Mall's acrylic dazzle of baubles
was only a tunnel under
the usual greedy street
where I drifted with other dreamers
in our land of mannequins,
forgetting what I came to buy,
twisted in the baffling wash
of fantasy. Twice a woman tugged
at my line of sight
until in a candy store
her hand idling on the nape of her neck
turned all enticements to fluff
that blew away in the small breeze
of her stride. Fool, I thought,
and bought a bag of jujubes
for old times' sake, as if I were hunched
in the flickering hall of forbidden films.
At the end of the concourse
I mounted the clacking stairs
and she was above me, light
of day shining gray in the slit
of her parted thighs.
I climbed the climbing steel,
she glided toward the glaring world
of all our concrete cares,
her sideways glance displaying
the face of my former wife.
My vexed heart smashed against
the limits of its caged desires
where I pace back and forth
chafing raw the flesh of an old rub.

Speedboat

By the shores of a Huron
sumptuous with planting and preening
I lean in the boathouse on foggy mornings
over still water to admire the lines
of chrome and lax flag on the stern—
wondering how someone could name
a boat for a maimed brother,
lost son who stifled his anger
at a tyrannous father by hurling
himself into silence.
Remnant of The Twenties, casual
in ascot and baggy ducks
you haunt the driver's seat
till your face recedes into cracked leather,
pale hand is only the glint
of a dissipating sun.

The first waves ripple in
from the open lake, the last bats
chitter into the eaves, and I perch
on the seat I never dare
to occupy with power.
Mews of gulls are muted
by the mossy roof, first clatter
of someone in the kitchen announces
soon another summer's day will launch us
paddling into reeds and wind.
I grip the hard rim returned
from its dark plummet down
the damp trough of night, guess
at the speed of your reckless dash
toward waters no one charts,
the shock of the reef you knew
was waiting. For those few moments of open
throttle, water and sky and air

deep as an unremembered dream,
did you hold the endless future
like this wheel, still and cold
and steering itself forever?

Family History

Often when you wake,
hands groping on objects
that should be familiar,
you hardly know us.
"Look, Granny, we've placed
your chair by the window."
What are they for, your frown says,
this vase, sunlight,
spiralled shell on the sill?
Sometimes a lucid phrase shines
out of you as brightly as ever,
but soon you shake the table,
spilling an iris
into a smear of purple.

Children try to lose the pails
we carried years ago,
straps of white appear on their backs
like slats of moonlight,
and each of us pretends
we are rocked safely
in the arms of recurrence.

On the last night even a moon arrives
to sift through the screen
on a porch where we gather
late and laughing, later and rocking—
uncles, aunts, and cousins—forms
unknown unless speaking.
You sit but your silence
passes among us,
shadowy figure touching our lips
with a gentle finger.

Soon I will not know you,
none of my stories will be told
by the voice that gathered
all of you year by year.

Someone begins,
and for hours we tell all we remember
of houses and children and small adventures.
Over the dunes and its grasses a wind
is repeating the sea,
and we chant our beginnings,
refusing to let you take them away.

Writer at Work

This is the summer
for painting a house,
for breaking the peace of our days.
Through seven years I have lived with walls
that shed their chips toward
the colors of other lives.
Doors and shutters are crazed and cracked,
the chimney needs pointing,
and rubbish of strangers is heaped under porches.
Up with ladders, the clanking of hooks on rungs,
the angry squeal of scraping
back to raw wood.

Wife and children cannot think,
the windows gape, insects click
their chitinous heads on ceilings and walls.
I cling and tremble at reeling heights,
twist a spine that will not unbend
and eat the flakes from soffits.
Under the porch I crawl in remnants
of lives I think I have never known—
tricycle tires, a skier's glove,
broken lumber, screens, and the headstone
of Sister Mary Bernard. I chuck all this
in a mound, haul away
to leave simple dust.

In dreams I claw the air,
topple and swarm down clapboards,
until I sink deep through layers of talings.
My hand fits that glove,
those wheels once rolled me through friendless yards,
and Sister, you are my sister,
the woman I might have been.
Again and again I chant old songs,

charms for the new, wet skins of birth.

Then silence. The smooth back and forth
of strokes that heal. Inside
my family hears only the lapping of hands,
a blind man groping his way home.

Brook Changes

I stand far up the stream
at the first lucid pool where every stone,
each rippling fold becomes a trout.
I pray against snags on leaf or rock,
stare into water, bend forward
taut along my sides—

and merge from feet to unblinking eyes,
a single sinew leaning against currents
in the lee of a stone. A bristled scrap
fights its fall on dazzled surface,
I lunge and am dragged against
a downswirl of water, my mouth
ripped upward into light.

At evening I kneel by the trapped pool
in a quiet bend, pause to regain
my familiar flesh. Against my side
a fish leaps in the slime of dead brothers.
I cut the lure from its lethal strand,
break the rod,
and plunge my hands into water
cold to the marrowbone.

Vacant Lot

You have lived in this city
long enough to see
how it shifts and turns.
Buildings drop in ashes,
wrecking balls splinter the wall
of some brotherhood or other.
Business trudges in and out.
Names in brick are contradicted
by brave new languages of signs.

But one morning you walk past
the deep pit never filled
after melted beams and stone
were carted off. Here is the place
where vacancy builds its home
of papers dropped by wind,
of lintels, tilted rubble, roots,
sandbank and gravel of an ancient river,
scree, snow-drifts on bedrock,
talings of grinding stars.

The freight train by the lake
shunts and heaves. Your bare hand
grips a mesh of steel, you breathe
the thin gray air of March
that always returns to feed
the blood of generations
and wonder at the persistent
attitude of love.

Voice in the Sky

The mad have entered my city.
By day they search corners of the sky
for things they have lost, their feet
jerk down to remind us how earth
is in constant motion
and no one is safe.

At night they walk searching
for a door that closed years ago.
They howl in the tongues of many species
warning of distant storms.
We rise clutching our sheets,
sweat drowning us from the grip
of holding on. In such slipping-down dreams
we will not recall the words
when we wake again, only the scattered
vowels of a language we knew
before we settled this foreign land.

Whenever I watch a slow leak of dawn
I am the boy again who rose in dark
to carry news to my neighbors,
tossing the scrolls on doorsteps.
At the dead end of Garden Terrace
is the house where a woman
is kept in an attic.

She waits for me, and in that timid light
before the first bird dares to test a song,
she sends a high thin voice
to wind into me, spiralling down
and down beyond the place of forgetting:

"Save me. Save me. Save me."

Recreation Hour

When wind blows
flowers off the tree
they won't become apples.
Every night my father beat
my mother, sometimes me.

Before he went fishing
I'd watch him in the backyard
burying worms.
He's dead now.
She lives so far away
we never talk.

For years I've collected questions
from children who grew up:
why did they put my father on a train?
when was your brother dragged away at night?
how many bombs fell when your town was killed?

Teach me to paste petals onto trees.

Child's Play

Across the backyard snow
we drove our armies.
Saturday I was German
but this was Sunday,
your turn to click the heels
and use our model Luger.
Through hours of bloodless killing
we crumpled and rose
and flung ourselves on the palisades
of bushes. Only
harassed crows flapped
and croaked in the hemlock,
only the pale new moon
continued to roll around
to a different yard where
children lay piled,
bone on bone.

African Violets

for Lyn Camire Tisdale

We have pruned, repotted,
watered, even neglected
your gift of unfailing purple blossoms.
They survive, but beyond our walls
the gentle are being murdered
in airports or fields without wheat.
We are hostages held in this century
by all the histories of neglect
who rise at times from bending over
a stubborn and hidden plant,
blessing what tokens of love
we can keep. These darkly green
and furry leaves breathe with us
and wait for another slip of pale light
marking the boundary of day.

A Curse for Dictators

May you stand by the window
of your palace. The city burns.
Your helicopter waits
on the roof to twirl you
into exile. You feel sorry
for your people, the ones
you tried to make better
than they were. How sad
your friends must die,
sad no one understands you.
May you open your mouth
as if to orate again.

But your jaw will not close.
The air is a wedge
jammed between teeth, tongue
is a fist balled like a gag.
Your hands grip the sill.
May you scream
the howl of all agony—
a man whose eyes are gouged,
woman raped for the twentieth time.

Your mouth is driven so wide
surely the sinews will break.
Wail now like a child
who wears the torched skin
his life will not leave,
a mother who cannot forget
five bodies piled in the yard,
fragments of her own birth cries.

Your breath is gone,
into the gape of your mouth
rush waves of black space

from gaps between the stars,
from the trance of a prisoner
gripped in a shaft
where he cannot lie down.
May you bloat on emptiness,
your closed mouth leave no seams
in the pure wall of your flesh.
Live in the valley of silence,
listening forever
for one echo.

For Leviathan

to arn chorn

At dawn the first spout rises into light
and I slip over the side of my boat.
Now they come closer, my face is sprayed
by falling wrack. I dive and hear
the eery wail of mother and child.
Slowly they roll toward me,
wide flukes bending in gentle furlings.
She turns her huge eye to me, opening the way
to a core serene beyond all the stars,
and the great fin caresses my side.

I am weary of walking the land,
bitterly breathing the air of mountain and plain.
Surely if I flow through all the seas,
mingling with herds as they graze in clouds of plankton,
I will be washed as clean as I was before I lifted myself
in pride out of grass, defiance
of gravity stiffening my backbone.

III. Winter Voices

The Other

I have seen him walking
in every weather. He leans
into wind, his thin face
honed by sleet. He marks
the streets with a pace
that measures a life
on pavement.

What goads him on,
so unrelenting in its thrust?
He stalks the fringes of my dreams,
I wake and he walks on the edge
of each day. But if he should go,
striding into the hole
where landscapes close
and leave no scar, the harm
would be more than questions
when I cross the street and touch
the ragged fingers of his glove.

"Who are you? Where
have you come from, where
are you going? Tell me now."
He turns that face,
brother of all resemblances.
"I have seen you walking,"
he says, "in every weather,
leaning into wind."

Aeneas Through The Looking Glass

I thought the worst the gods
could devise was memory itself—
the way it floods the estuaries
of a waking mind, drawn across
fresh water of a new day
by the drag of guilt, a moon
of regret. Mother, I would have carried
you from the burning city also
had you settled for a human fate.
Why won't you let me forget
the stench of brave flesh after
the tearing by beak or hound,
the woman whose face and hips
still press me in dreams,
friends gone without cry
in the sudden clutch of waves?

Let me forget, let me
push the future ahead
in the labor of each blank day,
and if this founds a city
or brings my boy to stand
on firmer ground than heaving waves,
so be it. I will work
for destiny if you walk
behind me, cutting away
the last stone of my steps.

Instead today you lead me
to believe I am entering a temple
of this strange town, but
on its walls you paint
my own past, scenes
as familiar as the smell
of my body sweating.

I walk sideways down the long hall,
a crab, eyes blinking the water
as if sleet whipped them,
but how can I turn away
when gates, towers, trees of my childhood,
closets, swords, twisting stairs,
and cobbles are trapped in gesso.
See how Creusa clenches one last time
to heave the wide head down and out,
how Ascanias struggles
to find his first breath.

But how can I trust these works
of art? In every panel I search
but never see myself. That portion
of my eye is burned as if I gazed
too long at the sun. I strain
to assemble the figure who is me,
but all I see is the blur
of browridge, a body shape I wear
closer than a jut of helmet,
plume that dangles over the visor.

Where am I, Mother?
How can I ever know the torment
of history you say I must accept
if you are always shifting your shape
and never let me see my own?

Don Giovanni in Retirement

Tell those peasant girls
to quit singing under my window.
They think it's spring
but we always see
what we want to see.
It's enough that almond trees
insist on blooming again,
that sparrows will twitter
their pitiful dances
across my sill while I
and their indifferent females
watch. Plumage disgusts me,
or finches with straw
in their beaks, domestic toilers.
I remember those jesting words,
how the company laughed
everytime I said them,
To be faithful to one woman
is to be unkind to all
the others. Well said,
don't you think? The bon mot
still satisfies as much
as a good glass of wine—
the way it gathers
to syllables even before
you know what it means,
then flowers in space,
making those puppet listeners
gather your bouquet of words.
Almost as good
as the slow pulse of hips
that draws out a woman's moan
from that place where I know
the soul lives, deeper
than Plato's cave, the land

in her being so far away
I never reached it, and all
I received were those wordless
messages fluttering into
black air between us.
Oh, those voices, each timbre
so different, and echoing,
echoing night after night
in the empty chamber where I
was my own guest of stone,
the statue of all I had killed
in my precious, lonely self.
So tell those sweet ladies
a man in a wheelchair reading
a book doesn't care
for their baskets, their mocking
processions. I take my lean
pleasure in other sights.
Last evening I rolled to the window
to watch two rooks flap to a branch.
He whet his beak
and mounted her. She hunched
and blinked and he plunged
once or twice. Over. They perched
on different branches for separate
preenings. I laughed and clapped
them away. Applause
for the old devil
and his random lusting.
I ask you, my dear Commendatore,
whether all your stiff
moral posturings have brought you
more than that hollow voice
with which you argue?

A Winter

When you took me to Rome, I did not know
what to expect. The language, you said,
would come easily. I have tried,
and can talk my way home from across the Tiber.
You will love the crust of pizzas,
pale Frascati, and roasted chestnuts.
With fingers and nose and palate
I have accepted more than you mentioned.
I am the one who studied the birds in the gardens
and told you their names. I am the one
who memorized tales of the saints
and can show you their symbols.
At first, you listened. *Did you know*
that the sibyl foretold to Augustus,
I start, but you wander away and I speak to a column,
this jumble of time, Aracoeli. Every Friday
we come for Bach on the organ,
and the lit gold of America shines down
on us listening. I think of the magic Bambino
swathed in gaudy jewels, wideeyed
in that tiny chapel. Waiting.

You did not forewarn
that I would wake in our marble room
unable to touch you and drift back to sleep.
You and I lie apart with curtains of rain
drawn between us—no, it's only the sound
we can't walk through.
Did it start because we knew no one here
and found that was true of ourselves?
Whenever we meet someone you say, *Not this evening.*
Your work, you tell them.
But, my stranger, you write nothing.
I have stood by the crack of your door
and watched you stare at the window.

Even your hands do not move.
When we speak at dinner the words
only scoop out the hollows for silence.

As a fugue gathered all of its voices
I reached for your hand. You started
as if a bird had fallen dead in your lap.
Someone behind us hissed.
Preludes and fugues, toccatas and canons,
what is Bach doing in such southern baroque?
What are we doing in so much richness of air
and time, breathing thinly, bleeding out
through the broken twigs of our limbs?

This Friday you tell me to go alone.
In rain I walk up the long steps
slowly. I count them, turn to look back
at the drowning city. I could shriek
from this height, a sibyl, small figure
thrusting her hands at nothing.
But I will go into these ancient doors,
under the glare of victorious gilding,
the mismatched columns, mishmash of history.
My hands cannot clasp any belief
as I sift through each level,
curator of prayers.

Caretaker

I am the one who comes with wrench
and hammer, draining each sink and toilet,
nailing the windows shut.
U-joints clogged with hair,
a freezer smeared with spilled ice cream,
and dust under every mattress
are remnants of their bodies'
motions. I sweep and flush
and try not to think of what it means—
this pale sun pooled on a wicker chair,
glut of cold ashes in the hearth.
Even I will not see winter
mass against these walls, gnawing
the putty from old frames,
mining the ground with frost
to sink the pilings lower every spring.

But sometimes when it's done,
each nail bent to keep thieves out,
each mattress stacked and wrapped in plastic
to discourage mice, I wander
from room to room, a furtive guest.
I have propped a headless doll in one windowseat.
The drawing of a mountaintop with figures
named *Mommy, Daddy* reaching for the sun,
some moment celebrated like a prayer for more,
is lifted from the floor and gently laid
inside the desk. They will assume
their own care placed it so.

I will not advance this calendar
marked with the last week's scurry,
will not remove a note that wavers
as I pass, pinned to the corkboard—
"Don't forget the eggs." I hope they will return
to laugh, if they're still happy,

recalling how all those boiled eggs
waited for me on the second shelf.

They will never know these last rites,
the intimate winding down.
I stand in a room of draped encumbrances,
rolled rugs, bare quadrants of glass
where spiders spin hasty webs for the last flies.
I open the face of the clock
and watch the pendulum's bright bronze
reflect a swaying room of clotted light,
try to distinguish tick from tock,
and with a hand that tires of making silence
I hold it dead center in its path.
It quivers but will not swing again.
If only I could show them this—
my own gross hand, retreating arm,
a snout for face, and then a wall
of nothing when the clouds shift over.
I could tell them nothing
is a place where even a prayer
vanishes.

A Letter from Lois

Another day selling homes, another day
turning keys to rooms where sunlight
on bare floor reveals the past
in every stain and scratch, where the wife
shakes her head at the narrow kitchen,
the husband shrugs, and Albert wonders
Will they live anywhere together for long?
because they hardly talk to each other,
and maybe at the last place,
the old Folsom house with twenty acres,
Albert will stand as far away as he can
while they lean at each other,
voices heaved in anger.

He turns the key to his own house,
lifts his mail, and standing in the hallway
he can almost sell the place.
Wait till you see the rooms upstairs,
the empty beds where my kids
used to live, the huge four-poster Nora
made me buy with canopy heavy enough
to smother your dreams forever,
the closets still full of clothes she said
I could give to the Salvation Army
after they left me: two boys, a girl, a wife
and all the noises that filled the house
that Albert lived in but now merely
occupies. Sold. Sign here. And oh, yes,
I neglected to tell you, I come with it.
But don't worry, I'm quiet and regular
in my habits. A quick dinner, some TV.
I'm almost invisible. Don't mind me
if I tiptoe into your bedroom at night
to lay a hand softly on your head
or listen to the sound of your breathing.

I'm Albert, I'm harmless, and this was my home.

Bills. Coupons. Appeal from the Blind
for money he does not have. A lavender envelope,
small, clear printing. Lois Wills. He frowns,
checks the address to be certain
the letter is his. The name does nothing.
Did he ever sell a house to a Lois?
He can count his old girlfriends on one hand,
all of them paling when Nora arrived
and he was nineteen. A vine scrapes in the wind,
its torn leaves flutter like swirls of bats.
He turns on a light. How can a house
full of chairs, rumbling of furnace, look more vacant
than even the Folsom's, unused for five years,
where shards of plaster crack underfoot, where his selling voice
is a trapped bird bashing from wall to wall?
Hang up the raincoat, slip off the rubbers—
apparel the sun made useless all day.
He takes something out of the freezer
shaped like the usual dinner, forgetting
to turn on the oven. Albert moves on tired feet
to the room where guests used to stay,
safer than lying upstairs where a canopy
holds in the flapping thoughts of his body.

Dear Albert, I won't be surprised
if you don't remember Lois Wills
who I am sometimes. When I'm not,
I wouldn't be writing you. But listen.
When you were a child and I was older,
you and your parents lived upstairs
and we were under—my father, mother,
and sister Elsa. You probably thought
I didn't see you. Fifteen years seems

a lot to a child. I know. There's another one
like me who visits my body
and wears some name I mustn't repeat,
and she stayed little. Bigger than Elsa
but smaller than Lois now, and she weeps
and weeps when she comes because
sadness was what they gave her, made her
drink it slowly all day long, or pick it
off old trees outside the window
and take it to bed. But I'm Lois now,
and you used to ride your tricycle
under my window. Once you fell and I ran out
and took you into our bathroom and washed your knees.
Once you sat on the front of my sled
and we went too fast down the big hill,
tumbled together, hitting your chin on my head.
We didn't care. We laughed. You grew up
into someone who made heavy footsteps
on days when my body began to refuse
to let me out of the bedroom, when fear
began perching in all the branches
or laughed suddenly out of car windows
and I looked for deep closets, made mother
hang new curtains so no one could see me
weep when it rained.
                              I write to you now
because only you can save us.
I could tell the last time I saw you
before you married, before you never came back,
that you were a friend of the Savior Boy,
the One who sometimes shows me the clamshell
that slowly opens, the One who says I can do
what I want with my hands. But sometimes He scolds
and says I've betrayed. I looked at you once
when you didn't know and I stood on the lawn

walking our dog at night. Forgive me.
For weeks I let my hands go up through walls,
up the wires that carried light to your room
and I came even in dark to touch what I'd seen.

Albert hears the wind batter, his own house
settle once before harsh rain starts licking
his windows. He stares at the light.
Lois Wills wears her long overcoat,
the runners slip downward, her hands on his chest
as the long hill swoops by them.
Had he once been a child? She said so.
Lois and Elsa, the voices of women below him.

Help me, Albert, my friend, friend
of the Savior Boy. Father is killing us.
Slowly. For years the poison has been slipped
to me and my mother. Now she is lying in bed
laughing, pretending she knows us.
I'm next, but no one believes me. The pills began
long ago when we went to the doctor, a man
with an obvious beard, phony nose.
They said it would put my head together
but I saw them smile when we left.
I don't know how he did it to mother.
As for myself, I have proof by the fact
that whenever I throw the pills down the toilet
truth comes back and the Savior Boy helps me
be someone else so they can't find me—
father and all his nasty helpers.
When he wears his glasses, his eyes
get twice as big, and his mouth when he sleeps
sucks air. He needn't eat, invisible demons
fly over him, lower their long, thin breasts.
Help me, Albert. He's after the Savior Boy

and the place where the Boy makes wetness and light
deep under the earth. Father knows where
the lovely clams open and he'll hold them shut
forever. Write to me. Send me your hands.
I have a room in my house where you can live
and father will never know
until it's too late—Lois.

He places the letter under the lamp.
Mad, of course. Should he send it back,
addressed to her father? Surely he knows
by now. Probably happens often.
But where had she found him, how from the years
of her mind had she plucked him?
He stands, pads back to the living room.
Why is his heart thudding? He turns off the light,
listens to rain in gusts, the beat of a branch.
Go away, he tells her, leave me alone.
But they tumble and roll in the snowbank.
And that is his father blowing dust
from a book, his mother listening to opera
while snow piles up forever over the window,
roofs, the treetops no longer in air.
What does it matter, how can he care
if this woman is mad?
He climbs the dark stairs slowly,
he crosses a cracking hallway
and enters the room. Flicking of sleet,
a distant foghorn. *I owned this house,*
but you can have it. For nothing. I give you
the plumbing, the walls, the bushes. I am
Albert and scarcely forty. Don't look for me.
I'm sleeping tonight with my childhood.

Overture

When I raise the baton I consider
how silence might be extended.
How long would those poised violas
wait, how long will an audience
settle for merely breathing, the music of heartbeats?
But someone coughs, a chair seat slaps
in the balcony; the restless body continues.
Does my father in the front row
lift his head or is he still sunk
in his evening depression?
Listen, old man, let this allegro
enter your bloodstream.

No one else in our family would have him,
too far away or full of their lives.
He can't be left alone, I told them,
and the mocking silence of distance,
that hissing of space came back through the phone.
Well, what can we do? they would cry,
and follow with cadenzas of justification.
My wife rocks her cello, her bow sweeps cleanly.
My eyes trace her line's syncopations,
and only the three of us matter.
What do you hear, old father, hands in your lap?
When you sink beyond us
through eighty years of living
is memory only the turning of pages
where photos come unstuck
to flutter and pile at your feet?
Last night we woke when you stood by our bedside,
a stark form staring down with hands loose
by your sides. Your glasses had slipped
on your nose, tufts of hair were the crest
of wild headress. But your face when I led you
into your lamplit room was mild.

What did he want? she asked me later.
We whispered in dark like children.
I could not speak, my grief
like his, that weight without words
because nothing explains it.
I listened to night turning and turning
in treetops, I listened in pauses of wind
for an answer. *He said he came to see
if he knew us.*

We leave the exposition in a tangle
of woodwinds. We'll come to such strange
transformations of themes we thought we knew.
When I told my friend the flautist
something about this despair he said,
*I read about a mental disorder
where you lose your memory backwards
starting from where you are, and once
an old man wandered back to the age
of nineteen and had no idea he was sixty-seven.
They tried to shock him forward again,
stood him up to a mirror and said,
'Look, if you're nineteen why
is your hair gray, your face so lined?'
But he only wept and said to them,
'Something dreadful has happened to me.'
When they took the mirror away, he forgot.*

I bring him to all my concerts,
hoping Mozart or Brahms will fill the woods
of his enchanted isle before once again
it all turns to stone. He has taught me
not to expect more than what we are living—
quick moments of grace. We return
to old themes, but the instruments differ,

and we won't go as far from home anymore.
In this brief coda hear how the phrase
we thought was a useless scrap is lifted
and shimmers, descends into unbroken light
of a cadence. I hold my hands still
for the final beats, giving the silence
its due. Last notes are never sounded.
A rest fills the measure.

Ricochet

I always hit the bullseye
but war was over before
I had to prove how I could fire
only at targets.
I didn't know what to do
so I went to work for a bank,
standing all morning in lobbies
showing my gun to kids.
"He's a marksman," my wife told neighbors.
She needed to say I was more than a guard.
Once my boy opened a drawer,
played with bullets, and I had to whip him,
left welts on his thighs.
I hoped someday when he had a kid
he'd know those were scars of my fear
flailing at all the things
that might kill if he didn't take care.

After the accident I worked
for the place where they rent protectors.
Vera worried. "Whose bodyguard?"
I shrugged. "Killers," she yelled. "Crooks.
Politicians. If they need you, they're guilty."
I said you don't have to shoot first,
don't have to kill, wounding
will do. I learned how
to follow close to a shoulder
with eyes on pockets and nervous faces.
I'm the guy in the loose Hawaiian shirt
or sheeny tuxedo or double-knit plaid
in the picture's corner, the guy
who's never looking at the Person
everyone else came to see.

Nobody blamed me, but I never forgot.
They shouldn't build banks with marble.
I fired two shots at the punk
just to scare him, missing on purpose.
How could anyone else get hurt?
But a bullet was loose in a room of stone.
They say the shell was almost spent
when it hit the kid. Didn't kill her,
but she never woke up. She's still
living, still in a coma.
I send her flowers every birthday.
She's thirty. Wouldn't it have been better
if the bullet had gone in deeper
or I'd aimed for a bullseye and dropped the punk?
What the hell did God have in mind
when he gave me this talent
without the will to aim it at people?
My own luck never ran out. One war,
three hold-ups, a knifer, mad bomber.
Someone else always did the shooting.

The day I fired a gun in that bank
was the last I ever carried it loaded.
All those years I took my chances.
Wouldn't they be surprised, those bigshots
who paid for protection? All I hoped
was that someone would try it.
I would have seen his eyes jerking,
watched in slow motion the hand pull
from the raincoat the snub-nosed blast
I'd step into, wiping out sounds
of that mother screaming, the marble echoing
shot after shot.

Vera, she died. My son lives in Texas,
he's married, and we write each other.
My hand's just as steady as ever.
I've got a honey two doors down
who cooks my breakfast, doesn't ask questions.
Someday we've all got to die.

A Simple Death

When Miss Tate read,
she told us of a river
souls drank from in order to forget.
Resting my face on the deep-gashed desk,
I saw a herd of people, Jed and Parsons,
Miss Milledge and Stan Humes and everyone
I could recall in town from twelve years
scurrying through its streets—all dead
but standing, staring without words,
too much like cows by the fence in a summer dawn.
I watched them spread out on the bank, then kneel
and cup the water, drinking their faces slack,
bodies falling like old leaves into the lazy current
where they twisted and were gone.
Miss Tate woke me gently, the others laughed,
but I said to her open face, "They'll drown."
"Who Nathan?" "The dead," I answered
to that fading bank of the wide bend near Lamont
where currents are invisible but deep.
She always followed our dreams better
than our pranks. "They've nothing to fear.
Not from water, not from memory."

For years I did not think of her
until I stood one night at my window
watching the slow stars turn, the fifth night
without sleep. To ease my own dismay,
I wondered what Miss Tate had to forget
that she could put it so, or place such words
in the waking mind of a twelve-year-old.
My wife lay sleeping, willing to take pills,
the kind that only deaden for a while,
so when she woke her pain would not be lessened
by watching the long night slip into whitening sky.
Only an infant, so young and small

he did not seem to own a face yet.
All those nights, those afteryears
he was only a body held tight in fear
he'd slip through unaccustomed hands.
In dreams I hugged him and walked us to the shore.
Always when I stooped to fill a cup,
to help him join the others
since he could not do this on his own,
I failed to be accomplice, wanted those wide eyes
never to lose the blur we must have been.
Gladly I'd have drunk it for him,
forgetting the harsh cry Molly woke me with
that morning, forgetting how heavy flesh can be
when breath has left it.

We've had five children, grown,
gone off across the land so sturdy,
so wild with living that we almost pushed
the last one at the end to move,
to marry, take his flailing down the road.
Last summer Henry Switt's boy drowned,
and Parcham's daughter thought the world
was ending, so she cut her wrists.
What is our simple loss to those?
We fought back, loving nights
we did not care who heard us
crank the bed across a thin-walled room.

When they had grown and gone,
when they'd even begun to bring new versions
of their faces home, why did I have to stand
one afternoon, holding my rake
to watch leaves drift and scatter on dark green?
They flung me weightless to that desk,
its furrows on my cheek and Miss Tate calling

Nathan, Nathan, but not to me—
telling that infant's name
as if she'd read what was to come.
And Molly. Who brought her out the kitchen door
to stand there with her arms cradled,
staring at me? Both of us
touched by the same strange hand.

That night after we'd tossed the echoes
of our love into a house too large,
I told her of my river, and she spoke its name.
"It's Greek," she said, "a myth."
Her breath was slipping over my face,
I placed one hand on her hip,
her fingers trailed across my neck.
By the river's bank
the three of us crouch and wait.

Beyond Change

Old burlap bags piled
by the furnace. Cardboard boxes
stacked to make a wall.
I found this one morning
in my basement. A figure
had crossed the yard
at dawn, slipping uphill
before I could make him out.
Hard ground he walked
in our cold, bare season
of late fall. Fear is the easiest
part of what I live with,
a woman in a vacant house.

I stared at the way the bags
shaped to a curling body's
need. I never lock the cellar door.
Haven't I secretly hoped
he would return? He left
when I kicked him out,
maybe twenty years ago.
I lose track, but not of the shape
of emptiness, that wide
place I fall through
on certain nights. Or Sunday afternoons
when traffic dies, when all you see
from windows are neighbors
walking their dogs. A clean
sweep in my life, I wanted.
Got it. Couldn't take his booze,
the angry flailing when I was
whatever he made me out to be.
I heard once he'd been seen
in Albany. Once in Troy.
Or so friends said,

trying to see if I cared.
My house, and always was,
from my father. I rented
for a few years, quit that.
Hated their arguments,
TV laughter, cabbage soup.
He'd be as old as I am.
I wouldn't want to sleep
on concrete. But tough,
or liked to think he was.

I left the bags, closed
the cellar door. Welcome
to that place. But I listen
at night, certain I hear
scraping under the floor.
The furnace shudders off and on.
At supper I think *If I call out*
to him, promise not to talk,
will he sit here in the kitchen?
I don't care for words.
I'd put food on the table,
watch him eat. I won't look
at how his hands shake
or his mouth hangs loose.
Maybe I'd pass him a note.
We could go on like this.
You live in the spare room.
Come and go as you please.
That's better for me than another cat,
better for him than wandering
from one frost to the next.
Better than nothing heaped on memory.

But maybe it's only a boy,
a stray. This morning I saw
a ragged kid stealing a can
at the store. I didn't tell,
don't care. If he lives
in the cellar, I don't want to know,
can't use that part of the house.
"Don't go," I say once outloud
when I lie down in my bed.
I listen. The slightest sound
is enough to tell me he's there.
I pick a field I have known
and tree without leaves.
I count the branches backwards
to the single trunk, go down
to roots. I don't even know
if I ever loved him.

Ice Fisher

I pay out line until it slackens.
I'm not into catching anymore.
Used to tote a full pail
when I trudged home over the snow,
but I got sick of the taste
of perch, would give them away,
then quit. Besides, I don't know
the neighbors now. Never was
the tug and hauling in
and scraping scales that took me.
I like pounding together a shack,
hauling it out, then squatting
over the hole I bore,
alone with a patch of clear ice
and sometimes wind that scratches up
drifts on the walls. So now
I don't have to pay for bait.
Sometimes I wonder what fish think
of empty hooks, lead on a string
sinking to the coldest rock.
But they don't think. Nothing
behind those agate eyes.

One winter a truck fell through.
I was too far away,
heard the spin and whine,
went out to look, saw the ice
still giving, cab going last
where a window was half down,
a figure howling, gone.
I ran but couldn't get too close.
No one came up. I marked
the spot where already a skin
of ice was forming. Next day
it was zero again. Diver

went down, said the two men's
faces were at the window
waiting. Spring, when they hauled
the truck on a barge, they found
the door had stuck. But the worst
was later that winter day
when they sent the diver down
again to try for the bodies.
Trouble announced itself
in his slack rope. They tugged,
left it dangling, kept the hole
open, punched out others
in a widening circle. All night
they axed the ice, shone spotlights.
Only so much air in tanks.
By morning they gave it up.

Thing is, when you lose the rope
in the dark far under ice
and you panic for only a moment,
or say the cold has numbed
your brain before the shock
wakes you when you touch
your waist and miss the tether
and look around to see no truck,
just dull water and far above a grayish light,
you are lost in a world
with heavy lid between you and sky.
When your head beats against ice
you've met the limit. Your fists pound
until you remember to stay calm,
save the stuff on your back.
Swim slowly along, upside down,
hands groping. Here a brighter glow
seems hopeful, or a crack, but ice

can heave and flaw and mend
again to leave a scar, a window
you can't break. The light dims.
Finally everywhere is black.
You are free to move anywhere
but up. You can even scream.

They never found him. I dreamed
once that I cleared the ice
in my hut and he was staring up.
Between us the solid glass
had no flaws, not even trapped bubbles.
His mouth formed slow words,
I put my ear against the cold.
The side of my head grew numb.
Tell me, tell me, I tried to say
but nothing left my throat. When I looked
again I was looking up to myself
looking down and I flattened my hands
as he did. Palm to palm we turned
slowly with ice between us.
I could tell no difference.

In summer I pay no mind
to the lake. Let them sail or whip
their skis into spray. I see
the waves. I see the sun fall down.
I'll even walk to the pier to watch.
Who talks to an old man feeding gulls?
All I'm saying is that winter
in my shack with an empty line,
no one to trouble me,
the lake as still as it can be,
I'm almost there.

Mr. Dibble Stands By The Gate

Hello, there. You're the young
couple from up the hill, aren't you?
Don't mind me, I only wanted
to say good morning. Fine day
for a walk, if you don't mind wind.
Tricky when it shifts around—
at least for an old fellow
like me. That your baby? I heard
you'd had one. He takes it all
in, don't he? It's the sun
that makes a day like this
worthwhile. You'd hardly know winter
was coming, except by the leaves
blown every way. See that broken
limb? Came down last night.
I'm Harry, 'case you wondered, live
here with Helen. Takes care
of me good for no reason
but kindness. I've no family.
Had to sell my house, gray one
down by the field. Couldn't
keep it up by myself.
You probably don't see me out
enough to even know I'm here.
Arthritis, rheumatism, you name it
I got a piece of the action.
That's why the cane, why
I lean like this all the time.
Say, look at him laugh
at those leaves flipped up.
It don't take much to keep them happy.
I was in the war, got some money
still comes. I give it to Helen.
She's off a lot at her store,
so I'm watching TV or reading papers.

Lived through almost every battle
they fought in France and some in Germany,
so this don't seem so bad,
except for having no one to call
my own blood kin.
I always wanted to marry, have kids.
You're lucky, little fellow like that
will mean a lot when you need to lean
and a cane don't seem enough
to carry it all.
Have more. Don't mind this mouth
cranking on about your business,
but you can never know if one
will live, and they tell me
nothing's worse than living beyond
the life of your child. Helen never
had one either, and when her husband
Joe died, cancer it was, sudden
in that winter we never had snow,
she started taking in lodgers. Summer
mostly. Now there's me. You see
what I mean about the wind?
That last twist must've bounced
off the barn, or maybe it just can't
make up it's mind which way
to come or go. Want some advice?
Don't get old, or if you do,
don't expect anything to change.
It just gets more the way it was.
Some days I'll walk in the field
to watch the cows eat grass
and find myself choked up so I can't see
which path takes me home,
and others, all the songs I've known
come to me and I sing

as if I'm drunk on that vodka
we found in a German tank.
That baby knows. See, he's laughing
at nothing, bless him. Here. I just want
to touch that hair once. Thanks.
It turns pure gold in this sun,
don't it? Well, you'd best go on.
I'm the one with the time to waste.
Helen, she won't be home till evening.

Preparing to be Happy

I am only an old woman who cannot sleep,
who sits in a chair by her bedroom window
high in the trees. The silk of my nightgown
slips over skin with my breathing.
How many years did I squeeze out the present?
I worried over the past—
Jacob's shirt unironed, the letter owed to Daniel,
the call I didn't make before my father died;
and built a hard wall of future—
the hope for an end to a war, wish
to have Jacob wake without pain.
Where did they go, those moments
I lived through without being there?

This evening at dinner, my skirt tucked
neatly, pillow plumped and all the family
squabbling toward dessert, I interrupted
my son Daniel whom I sometimes now
call Jacob—after all, since his father died
where is the name to go, aren't I ever
to use it again?—made his boys pause
in their teasing of sisters, a thing
they're too old to do. "What, Gramma?"
Sometimes I think Daniel evades me
by calling his mother Gramma as if
he could be his own son. "I want to tell you,"
(and I was not stopped by Tod whispering to Emmy,
"Oh no, another of Gramma's stories,"
do they think I'm deaf?) "that right now
what we're all doing is thinking
we're living, but none of us really is here
because we can't hold for even the second
it goes by us the thing that's slipping
through our minds when we try to think
of nothing but being right here."

Sheila was bringing the cake,
singing her tuneless soprano, and the kids
took the cue from their mother, bawling
my birthday out to every room of the house
and beyond to the neighbors. "Interesting,"
Daniel said, "now blow it!" "What is?"
Sheila asked, and Tod took a swipe with a finger,
was slapped on the top of the head by his mother.
But he's nineteen so the gesture
was pure nostalgia. Seven candles,
one for each decade. I wished, breathed in,
and blew—and left one fluttering.
"You'll have to wait another ten years,"
said Emmy, and I told her to cut.

"What did you wish?" Emmy asked
when she came upstairs to say goodnight.
She's eighteen and full of wishes,
has a boyfriend who tries to be polite.
But she's my favorite, and before I could tell her,
None of your business, she kept on talking.
"What did you mean at dinner?"
I was propped in my chair by the bed,
book closed on one finger to keep the place
where the old count was coming down from his tower
at last, and his horse was waiting.
"What I meant wouldn't make any sense to you now
but will later, and when it does it won't
make any difference because in the place
where you know it, regret will come instead,
the wishing you'd known when it could
have made you peaceful. So go on down."
I ended my riddle, saw by the jerk of her eyes
she'd also heard his car in the driveway.
But she's the one who knows what I mean

even when she doesn't know she knows,
so her eyes went steady, and her arms
surrounded me, face on my face, a whisper,
"Happy birthday, oh Happy Birthday, dear Gramma."
I knew those eyes glistened with pure expectation—
which does not cheapen our love or that moment.

I would hear Jacob stoking the furnace,
no voices from any child's room, and if there was peace
in the slow strokes of my brush through hair,
it came from foreseeing how this could be
one of those nights we would lie in the moonlight
and spread out our lovemaking slowly, slowly.
But if nothing happened that way, I was vexed.
Fool. I drowned that peaceful space as I waited,
flooding the simple moment with wishes
but draining the future empty.
Wasn't there plenty in the untangling strokes of my brush,
the scrape of shovel, a house full of all I loved?

I turn out my light,
place my book on the pillow
and sit by the window. How long?
When time stops a measured ticking
I know what it's like to be tree or lawn
or hovering mind with no body.
Emmy, Emmy, what are you doing?
my silent voice chants.
I see them pass through leaves, dim shapes
floating in the yard of a town where
even buses have stopped moving.
I lean to the opening, they whisper.
By the trunk of the tree they heap their clothes,
on a circle of grass where the crocuses
bud in spring, they stretch the pale forms

of their bodies and make ghostly love.

Emmy, my love,
I will tell no one. This is our secret,
and don't you remember that wishes told
can never come true?
What are you thinking? Now
while you lie without moving, skin cooling,
his touch almost memory.

Freeze

We have passed the gate
of rusted lions rampant,
unhinged from tilted stone.
"I don't know whose estate
it was," you tell me.

Is that a voice that makes us pause?
Only an evening thrush
quavering downward.

Beyond a disconnected fountain
we remember the childhood game,
how we twirled and stumbled
into our poses on someone's lawn
and if we fell, we lost.

A sundial clogged with ivy,
a marble seat off its blocks.
Again a single cry so near
our hands grip,
seizing the stillness.

I tell you, "They must have been wealthy
and lived somewhere else." Or was it ours
and we have forgotten?

The descent through sycamore and oak
is broken by roots. "In fall,"
you say, "I sometimes don't know
which season I am in."

"I'm sure the garden path
did not come here," I answer.
The brook's stones are treacherous
with weeping moss.

On the other side we recall
how we heard voices
on our own lawn playing that game
before our children grew
and moved away.

Someone must be calling us,
tongue like a flaming sword.
But it's only the red slash
of clouds beyond a spruce
bent by prevailing winds.

How still we stand,
how long the shadows.

Carnegie Mellon Poetry

1975
The Living and the Dead, Ann Hayes
In the Face of Descent, T. Alan Broughton

1976
The Week the Dirigible Came, Jay Meek
Full of Lust and Good Usage, Stephen Dunn

1977
How I Escaped from the Labyrinth and Other Poems,
    Philip Dacey
The Lady from the Dark Green Hills, Jim Hall
For Luck: Poems 1962-1977, H. L. Van Brunt
By the Wreckmaster's Cottage, Paula Rankin

1978
New & Selected Poems, James Bertolino
The Sun Fetcher, Michael Dennis Browne
A Circus of Needs, Stephen Dunn
The Crowd Inside, Elizabeth Libbey

1979
Paying Back the Sea, Philip Dow
Swimmer in the Rain, Robert Wallace
Far From Home, T. Alan Broughton
The Room Where Summer Ends, Peter Cooley
No Ordinary World, Mekeel McBride

1980
And the Man Who Was Traveling Never Got Home,
    H. L. Van Brunt
Drawing on the Walls, Jay Meek
The Yellow House on the Corner, Rita Dove
The 8-Step Grapevine, Dara Wier
The Mating Reflex, Jim Hall

1981
A Little Faith, John Skoyles
Augers, Paula Rankin
Walking Home from the Icehouse, Vern Rutsala
Work and Love, Stephen Dunn
The Rote Walker, Mark Jarman
Morocco Journal, Richard Harteis
Songs of a Returning Soul, Elizabeth Libbey

1982
The Granary, Kim R. Stafford
Calling the Dead, C. G. Hanzlicek
Dreams Before Sleep, T. Alan Broughton
Sorting It Out, Anne S. Perlman
Love Is Not a Consolation; It Is a Light, Primus St. John

1983
The Going Under of the Evening Land, Mekeel McBride
Museum, Rita Dove
Air and Salt, Eve Shelnutt
Nightseasons, Peter Cooley

1984
Falling From Stardom, Jonathan Holden
Miracle Mile, Ed Ochester
Girlfriends and Wives, Robert Wallace
Earthly Purposes, Jay Meek
Not Dancing, Stephen Dunn
The Man in the Middle, Gregory Djanikian
A Heart Out of This World, David James
All You Have in Common, Dara Wier

1985
Smoke From the Fires, Michael Dennis Browne
Full of Lust and Good Usage, Stephen Dunn (2nd edition)
Far and Away, Mark Jarman
Anniversary of the Air, Michael Waters
To the House Ghost, Paula Rankin
Midwinter Transport, Anne Bromley

1987
Some Gangster Pain, Gillian Conoley
Other Children, Lawrence Raab
Internal Geography, Richard Harteis
The Van Gogh Notebook, Peter Cooley
A Circus of Needs, Stephen Dunn (2nd edition)
Ruined Cities, Vern Rutsala
Places and Stories, Kim R. Stafford

1988
Preparing to Be Happy, T. Alan Broughton
Red Letter Days, Mekeel McBride
The Abandoned Country, Thomas Rabbitt